HAWAI'I'S
CATCH OF THE DAY
Honolulu's Finest Seafood Recipes

Created and Edited by Kristine Vasey Smith

Mutual Publishing

Library of Congress Catalog Card
Number: 97-70287

First Printing May 1997

97 98 99 00 01 02

Softcover
ISBN 1-56647-143-5

Cover design by Kennedy and Preiss Design

Mutual Publishing
1127 11th Avenue, Mezz. B
Honolulu, Hawaii 96816
Telephone (808) 732-1709
Fax (808) 734-4094
e-mail: mutual@lava.net

Printed in Australia

Introduction

Fresh seafood has always been popular in the islands. Today Hawaii's consumption of fresh seafood is twice that of the United State's per capita average. In addition, Hawaii's per capita consumption of raw tuna is exceeded only by Japan.

There are four basic categories of fish available and popular in the islands. They are:

TUNAS
BILLFISH
OPEN OCEAN FISH
BOTTOMFISH

Tunas consist of Ahi, Aku and Tombo. All varieties of tuna are good for grilling and broiling. It is not recommended to steam or poach fish in this category. Ahi is the preferred fish for sashimi or sliced raw fish. Aku is preferred for poke dishes—chopped raw fish seasoned with shoyu, seaweed and green onions. Tombo, while considered too soft for sashimi, is preferred for gourmet smoked fish products.

In the billfish category Hebi, Kajiki and Nairagi are all good grilled, broiled, baked or sauteed. Kajiki is good for sashimi, and Nairagi is recommended for use in cold seafood dishes and salads. Don't steam any type of billfish.

All open ocean fish can be baked, sauteed or poached with great success, and Ono is also good broiled. Mahimahi is one of the more popular fishes of the islands due to its delicate almost sweet flavor. Opah is also delicious sashimi style

Bottomfish are best baked, steamed or poached. Don't grill, smoke, or dry any members of this category. Hapu'upu'u is best steamed and is the fish of choice by restaurants for sweet-sour or fishhead soup. Onaga is frequently used for oriental ceremonial occasions. Opakapaka and Ulua are considered good for sashimi.

When purchasing fish allow 3/4 lb. per serving if buying the whole fish. If fish is cleaned, 1/2 lb. per serving is sufficient.

Avoid purchasing fish with a pronounced fishy smell or with a dry look around the edges. Fresh fish is very perishable and should be refrigerated until ready to cook. Keep frozen fish frozen hard. Thaw slowly, overnight, in refrigerator.

Don't overcook fish as it will dry out and loose its taste. Fish is done when it looks opaque and flakes slightly when tested with a fork. When grilling, a moderately hot fire is best. Cook a whole fish 10-12 minutes per inch. Fillets will take 8 minutes per inch of thickness to cook. Turn once half way through the appropriate time except when the fish is less than one inch thick. In this case, cook on one side only.

Pupus

Crab Dip

Doris Harrison

2 8 oz. pkg. cream cheese
2 6-1/2 oz. cans of crab, drained
Dash garlic powder
1/2 cup mayonnaise
2 tsp. prepared mustard
1/4 cup dry Vermouth
1 Tbs. minced onion
Seasoning salt to taste

Combine all ingredients in a saucepan. Heat until cheese melts and sauce is smooth. Season to taste. Serve in a chafing dish with crackers or toast points.

Hot Crab Dip

Bonnie Louise Judd

8 oz. cream cheese
1 cup Bernaise sauce (Knorr Mix)
1 can crabmeat, drained
8 oz. imitation crabmeat
1 Tbs. lemon juice
1 Tbs. dehydrated onion
1 clove garlic, minced
Lemon pepper, Thyme, Tarragon and Cayenne to taste
Toasted sliced almonds for garnish

Combine all ingredients except almonds in a saucepan. Heat, stirring constantly until mixture is smooth. Serve hot topped with almonds with crackers or petite ryes.

Ono Avocado and Crab Dip

Jan Weidner

1 medium avocado
4 oz. cream cheese
1/2 cup crabmeat
Salt, pepper and Tabasco sauce to taste

Soften cream cheese. Peel avocado and mash. Mix with cream cheese. Mix in crabmeat and seasonings. Serve with crackers or vegetables.

Salmon Pate

Jeff Cross
General Manager, Hard Rock Cafe Honolulu

1 7-1/2 oz. can salmon
11 oz. cream cheese
1 small onion, minced
1/2 t. liquid smoke
Juice of half a lemon

Drain salmon, discard skin and bones. With a hand mixer, combine all ingredients and mix well. Serve in a crock with better crackers and petite rye.

Mexican Shrimp Dip

Bonnie Louise Judd

1 cup sour cream
1 cup Mexican salsa
1 can shrimp, drained
3 Tbs. minced cilantro

Mix all ingredients in a bowl. Chill. Serve with blue corn chips.

Dilled Shrimp Spread

Joy Weeman

1 4-1/2 oz. can shrimp, drained
1 8 oz. pkg. cream cheese, softened
1 Tbs. mayonnaise
1/4 to 1/2 tsp. garlic powder
1 Tbs. catsup
1-1/2 tsp. Worchestershire sauce
1 tsp. lemon juice
2 Tbs. grated onion
1 tsp. dill seeds

Combine ingredients 2 thru 9. Stir in shrimp—mix well.
Garnish with reserved shrimp and dill seeds.

Salmon Spread

Edwina Kaapana

7-3/4 oz. can Alaskan salmon
4 oz. whipped cream cheese
2 tsp. onion flakes
Tabasco or Worcestershire sauce to taste

Drain salmon. Add cream cheese and blend until smooth.
Blend in seasonings. Refrigerate at least 2 hours or
overnight.

Serve with rye or pumpernickel bread. Makes one cup.

Crab Spread

Debbie Simpson

1 can crabmeat, drained
1 small bunch green onions, chopped
1 pkg. grated Mozzarella cheese
1 small can chopped olives, drained
Mayonnaise to taste

Mix all ingredients together. Spread on french bread and toast until cheese melts and becomes browned.

Calamari Provencal for Two

Executive Chef Paul N. Kerner
Nicholas Nickolas

1 oz. olive oil
1 cup Squid Calamari, cleaned and sliced in 1/2 inch pieces
3 Tbs. butter
1/2 Tbs. minced garlic
1 tsp. Lea & Perrin Worchestershire sauce
1/2 tsp. Tabasco sauce
1 cup beef broth, thickened with cornstarch to medium
   consistency
1 cup diced tomatoes
1/2 cup Parmesan cheese
1 tsp. oregano

In a large saucepan, heat oil to medium-high temperature until almost smoking. Sear Calamari quickly. Add butter, garlic, tomatoes and oregano. Add beef broth. Add Tabasco and L & P Worchestershire sauce. Add grated Parmesan cheese.

Pacific Broiler Grilled Shrimp and Scallops

Kono Wong, Owner and Chef
Pacific Broiler

8 shrimp (16/20 count)
8 scallops (16/20 count)
8 bamboo skewers
2 Tbs. melted butter
4 oz. linguine
1 Tbs. olive oil
1 clove garlic, minced
2 tsp. chopped parsley
Tamarind Sauce
Tomato-Basil Avocado Salsa
Lemon wedge and basil sprig for garnish

Secure a shrimp and scallop on each skewer. Brush with melted butter and grill over low flames of kiawe wood charcoal until done. Cook linguini as directed on package, drain. Add olive oil, parsley and garlic; toss lightly and divide between four individual plates. Top with grilled seafood. Accompany with sauces and garnish with lemon wedge and basil sprig.

Tamarind Sauce:
1 pkg. (16 oz.) preserved tamarind
2 cups water
2 Tbs. vegetable oil
1 clove garlic minced
1/2 tsp. minced serrano or jalapeno chili
3/4 cup sugar

Combine tamarind with water and mix well using your hand until water is absorbed. Press pulp through a strainer. Heat oil in skillet and saute garlic and chili. Add strained tamarind and simmer for a few minutes. Add sugar and simmer 10-15 minutes, stirring occasionally. Cool. Makes 1-3/4 cups

Tomato-Basil Avocado Salsa:
1 cup diced avocado
1 to 1-1/2 Tbs. fresh lime juice
1/4 cup chopped tomato
1/4 cup diced onion
2 Tbs. chopped fresh basil
1 serrano or jalapeno chili, minced
Salt and black pepper to taste

Place avocado in small bowl and pour in lime juice. Add tomato, onion, basil, chili, salt and black pepper; blend well. Place avocado seed in center of salsa until ready to serve to prevent discoloration. Refrigerate. Makes 1-1/4 cups

Kani No Nori Age Tempura

Gary Yoshinaga

1/2 lb. imitation crab
1/4 cup green onion, minced
1/4 cup celery, minced
1 raw egg, beaten
2 Tbs. mayonnaise
1/4 cup breadcrumbs
Dash each of shoyu and salt
6 sheets Yaki Nori

Thaw crabmeat and shred into a bowl. Add green onion, celery, egg, mayonnaise, breadcrumbs, shoyu and salt. Mix well. With your hands squeeze out any excess liquid and transfer remaining crab mixture to another bowl. Discard excess liquid. Divide into six equal portions. One at a time, lay "Nori" seaweed on a cutting board. Distribute one portion of the crab mixture evenly along the lengthwise end of "Nori". Roll until you almost reach the other lengthwise end. Moisten this edge slightly with water and continue rolling, sealing the edge. Pour enough cooking oil in frying pan to attain depth of about 1/2 inch. Heat and quickly fry rolls until they "firm up". Immediately remove from oil and drain for a few minutes on paper towel. Do not overcook. If allowed to fry too long, seaweed will split. Cut each roll in thirds diagonally, serve, and eat with a smile!.

Wok Magic Prawns

Bones Yuen, Chef
Serendipity

5 pound live Hawaiian freshwater prawns
4 cups salad oil
Fresh ginger, thumb size; peeled, julienne 2-1/2 inches
Oyster sauce, good quality, about 3/5 of a bottle
3 shots of sweet scotch (Black Label or Cutty)
One bunch green onions, julienne 2-1/2 inches
Wok and tools
Big bowl, tongs, corn starch
Kindling

This dish is done over a fire in a Wok. It is fast and you should be very careful or you could end up with singed eyebrows. In the big bowl, toss live prawns with cornstarch using the tongs. Coat the prawns thoroughly. Heat Wok until smoking. Throw in prawns and oil (hot Wok, cold prawns, cold oil). Toss until 1/2 red (1/2 cooked) adding more oil if needed. Add ginger and toss. Add scotch—stand back, it will "fwoomp". Add oyster sauce and toss. Add green onions and toss. Remove Wok from fire. Turn onto platter and serve.

Lobster Bites

Kris Smith

2 lb. lobster tail, steamed and chopped coarsely
5 doz. Belgian Endive leaves, cleaned and trimmed

Sauce:

1 cup mayonnaise
3 Tbs. honey
2 Tbs. minced green onion
1-1/2 Tbs. lemon juice
2 tsp. curry powder
3 Tbs. ketchup
1 tsp. Mrs. Dash

Paprika

Combine all sauce ingredients in a bowl and mix well. Fold
in lobster chunks. Place a spoonful of mixture on the base of
each endive leaf. Sprinkle lightly with paprika. Serve.

Shark Bites

Kris Smith

4 Tbs. butter
1/4 cup Balsamic vinegar
1 lb. shark fillet, cut into 1 inch strips
1 yellow bell pepper
1 red bell pepper
1 medium Maui onion
Manoa lettuce leaves
Macadamia nut bits

Clean and slice peppers and onion into strips. Melt one tablespoon of butter in a skillet and saute peppers and onion until soft. Remove from pan with slotted spoon. Melt remaining butter and add vinegar. Stir. When mixture begins to bubble, add shark strips. Cook over medium heat for about five minutes, turning once. Remove from pan with slotted spoon and transfer to serving platter. Return pepper/ onion mixture to pan and coat with sauce. Transfer to plate. Serve with lettuce leaves and macadamia nut bits. To assemble: Take one lettuce leaf, top with shark strip and one tablespoon pepper/onion mixture. Sprinkle with macadamia nut bits. Fold lettuce leaf around strip to enclose and eat.

Bon's Blackened Fish

Bonnie Louise Judd

2-3 A'u or Ahi steaks - 1/2 to 3/4 inch thick
1 tsp. powdered wasabi
1/2 tsp. ground cumin
2 Tbs. chili powder
1/2 tsp. lemon pepper
1/2 tsp. granulated garlic
1/8 tsp. cayenne pepper
1/2 tsp. thyme leaf
2 Tbs. peanut or safflower oil
Salsa / Shoyu and wasabi dipping sauce
Cilantro

Mix all spices together on a dinner plate and dredge fish
covering all outer surfaces. Preheat a heavy cast iron
frying pan for five minutes on high. Add 2 Tbs. oil to pan
immediately before cooking fish. Be prepared for the oil to
smoke a lot. Reduce heat to medium high after you add fish
to pan. Cook just one minute on each side. Spices will
become a blackened crust. Slice into strips, garnish with
cilantro and serve with salsa and/or wasabi dipping sauce.

Stuffed Mushrooms

Kris Smith

2 dozen medium to large mushrooms
1 can crabmeat, drained
1 Tbs. minced green onion
1 cup grated Swiss cheese
1/2 cup mayonnaise
1 tsp. lemon juice
1/4 tsp. curry powder
1/4 cup Italian bread crumbs
1/4 cup melted butter

Clean mushrooms thoroughly, removing stems. Combine remaining ingredients, except melted butter, and mix well. Stuff center of each mushroom with spoonful of crab mixture. Arrange mushrooms in baking pan, dribble with melted butter and broil for 5-10 minutes or until stuffing is golden brown and puffy. Serve while still warm.

Tofu and Seasoned Clams

Connie Young

1 block tofu, cubed
1 can seasoned clams
2 Tablespoon shoyu
1-1/2 Tablespoon sugar
1 Tablespoon water

Mix together in a wide saucepan the shoyu, sugar and water. Bring to boil and add tofu and seasoned clams. Simmer 5 minutes and serve.

Tuna Mold

Beverly Seman

1 can tuna (packed in water), drained
2 3-oz. pkg. cream cheese, softened
1 cup mayonnaise
1 tsp. lemon juice
1/2 cup minced onion
1 can cream of asparagus soup
2 envelopes unflavored gelatin dissolved in 4-5 Tbs.
*   hot water*

Mix together first five ingredients. Combine soup and
gelatin mixture, blend well with cream cheese mixture.
Pour into well greased jello mold.

Chill 4-5 hours or overnight. Unmold and garnish with
olives, pimentos or celery leaves. Serve with wheat crackers
or rye rounds.

Lobster Rumaki

Kris Smith

Lobster Tail Meat
Sliced water chestnuts
1 lb. bacon strips, cut in half

Marinade:
1/4 cup shoyu
1 Tbs. oyster sauce
1 Tbs. sake
1 tsp. minced garlic
Dash of Chinese Five Spice

Cut raw lobster into 1 inch chunks. Combine all marinade ingredients and add lobster chunks. Let sit 15 minutes. Take one chunk lobster, one slice water chestnut and roll up in raw bacon piece. Fasten with a toothpick. Broil until bacon starts to crisp. Serve hot with shoyu for dipping.

Ricotta Crabmeat Fritters

Nathan Kaolani Copper

1/3 cup butter or margarine
1/2 cup sugar
2 eggs, well beaten

Cream butter and sugar. Mix well with beaten eggs. Sift into this:

2 cups flour
3 tsp. baking powder
1/2 tsp. salt

Mix well.
Add *1 cup milk* and mix well.

Fold in *1-1/2 cup Ricotta cheese*
1/4 cup crabmeat, flaked

Drop from tablespoon into hot oil. Fry until golden. Sprinkle with powdered sugar and serve warm.

Limu Aku Poke

Hannah and Jimbo Beaumont

Fresh Aku
Hawaiian Salt
Limu-Kohu (red feather seaweed)
Manauwea (OGO-crunchy stick seaweed)
Red Chili Peppers
Chili pepper water
'Inamona (kukui nut paste)–1/2 tsp. per 1/2 lb. fish

Dice aku into 3/4 inch cubes. Season with Hawaiian salt.
Add equal portions of chopped manauwea and limu-kohu.
Finely mince 1 or 2 small chili peppers. Add chilies and
'Inamona to fish/seaweed. Mix all together (lomi). Add
chili pepper water to taste. Refrigerate covered for at least
two hours.

Smoked Salmon

Kris Smith

Mix 2 quarts water with 1-1/4 cup Hawaiian salt and 2-1/2 tsp. liquid smoke. Add cleaned whole salmon. Cover and refrigerate for four days. Remove from liquid, slice thin and serve with cream cheese and capers.

Spicy Shrimp

Kris Smith

5 lb. large shrimp or prawns, cooked and shelled
2 cups olive oil
1-1/2 cups cider vinegar
1 large bottle capers
1 Tbs. Mrs. Dash
2 tsp. Tabasco

Arrange shrimp in large baking pan. Combine remaining ingredients.

Pour over shrimp. Marinate 12 hours. Transfer shrimp to bed of lettuce and serve.

Soups & Salads

Crab Soup

Matthew Cabot

2 Tbs. butter or margarine
1 medium size onion, chopped
3 Tbs. cornstarch
2 quarts low-fat or whole milk
1 8 oz. bottle clam juice
1/2 cup dry sherry
1 tsp. Worcestershire sauce
1 lb. shelled cooked crab
1 hard cooked egg or 3 hard cooked egg yolks, rubbed
    through a fine strainer
Salt and pepper

Melt butter in a 4-5 quart pan over medium heat. Add onion and stir often until golden, 10-15 minutes. Smoothly mix cornstarch with about 1/4 cup of the milk, then add mixture along with remaining milk to the pan. Stir often until mixture boils; turn heat to medium-low and add clam juice, sherry, Worcestershire and crab. Stir gently until hot. Ladle into bowls. Sprinkle with egg and salt and pepper to taste.

Makes about 3 quarts or 8-9 servings.

Seaside Chowder

Millie Sohl

1/2 cup chopped onion
2 Tablespoon butter or margarine
1-24 ounce can V-8 or 1 can tomato paste cut with 4 cans
    water
1-10 ounce box frozen cut green beans
1 teaspoon salt
1/8 teaspoon hot pepper sauce
1 pound fish fillets, cut in 2 inch pieces

In large saucepan, cook onion in butter until tender. Add
remaining ingredients, except fish. Bring to boil, and cook 5
minutes, stirring occasionally. Add fish and cook 10 minutes
more or until fish is done.

Serves 4.

New England Clam Chowder

Gary Remus

1 lb. fish fillets <u>or</u>
2 cans minced or chopped clams
3 bacon strips, diced
1/2 cup chopped onion
2-1/2 cups diced potatoes
1-1/2 cups boiling water
1 tsp. salt
Dash pepper
2 cups milk
1 Tbs. melted butter
Parsley sprigs

In a frying pan, cook bacon pieces until crisp, add onions and cook until tender. Add potatoes, water, seasonings and fish or clams. Cover. Cook slowly for 15-20 minutes or until potatoes are tender. Blend in milk and butter. Cook until well heated. Garnish with parsley sprigs. Each serving can also be sprinkled with a dash of paprika for added taste.

Serves 6

Seafood Chowder

Gary Remus

6 slices bacon, diced
1 cup chopped onion
1/2 cup diced green bell pepper
1/2 cup chopped carrots
1/2 cup chopped celery
2 cups diced potatoes
1-16 oz. can tomatoes, chopped with liquid
2 cups clam juice
2 cups fish, cut into 1/2 inch cubes
1/2 tsp. oregano
1 tsp. marjoram
1 bay leaf
Salt and pepper to taste

Fry bacon; saute onion, pepper, celery and carrots. Stir in remaining ingredients. Simmer for 30 minutes.

Serves 6.

Each serving can be topped with one tablespoon of chopped fresh parsley.

Oyster Stew

Joan Evans

In the chill section of the market, select two jars of oysters. Cut them in halves or quarters. Lightly brown a crushed garlic clove and 2 minced medium onions in 3 Tbs. butter, discard garlic husks. Put 1 quart rich milk (or half and half) into double boiler to heat, add onions and cook until tender. Put oyster & liquid in saucepan and heat with a little salt, cayenne, and a bay leaf. Just before oysters are curled turn into the milk/onion pot. Stir in 1/2 cup dry white wine. Cook oysters a minute longer and serve with a ring of finely chopped parsley and scarlet petals of paprika.

Serves 6.

Bouillabaisse, Hawaiian Style

Kris Smith

1/4 cup olive oil
1 large onion, chopped
3 tsp. minced garlic
32 oz. clam juice
3-1/2 lb. canned stewed tomatoes
Peel of one orange

1/4 tsp. saffron
1/4 tsp. fennel seed
1/4 tsp. thyme leaves
2 bay leaves
1/8 tsp. fresh black pepper

4 each Hawaiian slipper lobster tails
1 lb. frozen mahimahi fillets
1 lb. red snapper fillet
1/2 lb. scallops
1/2 lb. prawns

Saute onion and garlic in oil until onion is transparent. Add clam juice, tomatoes, orange peel and spices. Bring to boil. Reduce heat and simmer, covered for one hour, stirring occasionally. Cool and refrigerate overnight, covered. Wash fish and cut fillets into bite size pieces. Cut lobster tails (in shell) in half crosswise. Heat stock to boiling. Add lobster tails and prawns. Reduce heat and simmer 4 minutes. Add mahi and snapper and simmer another 5 minutes. Add scallops and simmer another 5 minutes. Serve with garlic bread and green salad.

Serves 6.

Royal Alii's Avocado Salad

Smoki Foods of Hawaii, Inc.
Alii Seafoods

1 Ripe Avocado
4 ounces Alii's Hawaiian Smoked Salmon
1/2 cup fresh cream
1 shot Hawaiian rum
Dash Tabasco
Dash Worchestershire sauce
1/4 head Iceberg Lettuce or Romaine Lettuce, chopped
Black Pepper and Hungarian Paprika to taste

Halve and pit avocado. Mix smoked salmon, cream, rum, Tabasco, Worchestershire and chopped lettuce. Stuff avocado halves with mixture and season with pepper and paprika.

Serves 2.

Red Ogo Salad

Ernest K. Moses Jr.

1 lb. red Ogo seaweed
1 round onion
2 tomatoes
Rice wine vinegar, to taste

Cut onion into strips and tomatoes into small wedges. Clean,
blanche, and drain ogo. Mix with onions and tomatoes.
Pour rice wine vinegar over mixture, cover and refrigerate
24 hours. Serve cold.

Serves 4.

Celery Seed Dressing

Executive Chef William Teruya
Outrigger Canoe Club

3 oz. prepared mustard
Juice of one lemon
5 Tbs. sugar
1/4 tsp. pepper
1 raw egg
1 Tbs. pureed garlic
2 tsp. celery seed
1 Tbs. salt
3 cups salad oil
1/2 cup cider vinegar

Beat together with an electric mixer until fluffy the mustard, lemon juice, sugar, pepper, egg, garlic, celery seed and salt. Gradually add oil until well mixed. Thin out by gradually adding cider vinegar. Store in the refrigerator.

Makes 4 cups.

Editor's Note: This is my favorite marinade for fish fillets.

Poisson Cru

Kris Smith

2 lb. fish, cubed
1 Tbs. Hawaiian salt
Lime juice

Marinate fish in Hawaiian salt and enough lime juice to cover for at least 8 hours or overnight, tossing occasionally. Drain fish and set aside.

Mix together:
1/4 cup olive oil
1/2 tsp. crushed oregano
1/2 tsp. seasoning salt
2 stalks celery, chopped
1/4 tsp. pepper
1 medium Maui onion, chopped
1 medium cucumber, seeded and chopped
2 medium tomatoes, chopped

Fold marinated fish into this sauce. Meanwhile, thicken 3/4 cup canned coconut milk by heating for fifteen minutes on medium low heat. Allow coconut milk to cool. Fold into fish mixture. Chill and serve.

Serves 6.

Scallop Seviche

Kris Smith

1/2 lb. bay scallops (the small kind) or if only sea scallop
  are available, cut in half
3/4 cup fresh lime juice
1/4 cup fresh lemon juice
2 Tbs. extra virgin olive oil
1/4 cup diced Maui onion
1 tomato, peeled, seeded and diced
1 Tbs. chopped fresh coriander (or 1 tsp. if dried)
1 small cucumber, chopped
2 tsp. minced fresh cilantro

Mix lime and lemon juices. Add scallops and marinate
overnight. Toss with olive oil. Mix all vegetables. Fold in
scallops and serve.

Serves 4.

Swedish Herring Salad

Kris Smith

1 lb. pickled herring
2 potatoes, boiled and cubed
1 apple; peeled, cored and diced
1 small pickled cucumber, diced
1 small red onion, diced
2 cups pickled beets, diced
2 hard-boiled eggs, sliced
Sour cream

Cut herring into chunks. Mix with potato, apple, cucumber, onion and beets. Cover and refrigerate for at least four hours. Garnish with egg slices and serve with sour cream.

Serves 6.

Ika Salad

Yvette Paz

3 small packages dried shrimp
3 small packages soft saki ika (cut into 1 inch pieces)
1/2 cup white vinegar
1/2 cup vegetable oil
1 bunch watercress (rinsed and cut into bite size pieces)
2 medium firm tomatoes (cut into bite size pieces)
1 Maui onion (cut into slices)

Soak ika and shrimp in oil for one hour. Add vinegar and remaining ingredients except watercress. Chill for one half hour. Add watercress and toss. Serve.

Serves 10.

Crab, Macaroni and Potato Salad

Kris Smith

3 lb. salad potatoes
1/2 cup chopped celery
1/2 cup bottled Italian dressing
2 Tbs. sweet pickle relish
3 hard boiled eggs, chopped
1 cup mayonnaise
1 cup elbow macaroni
1 cup chopped onion
1 Tbs. prepared mustard
1 small can crabmeat, drained

Wash potatoes and cut into cubes. Cook in boiling water until done. Test with knife for doneness-potato cubes should be tender but not soft. Drain in colander. Cook macaroni and drain. Mix together. Add celery, onion and Italian dressing. Marinate overnight. Add remaining ingredients and mix thoroughly. The amount of mayonnaise used should be decreased or increased according to your particular preference. Sprinkle with paprika (optional) and minced parsley to add color just before serving.

Serves 12.

Pasta Salad

Kris Smith

One small bag tricolored twisted noodles, cook according to
*   package directions*
1/2 onion, finely chopped
2 carrots, peeled and sliced thinly
2 cups broccoli flowerettes
1 small zucchini, sliced thinly
1/3 cup Lea & Perrins White Wine Worcestershire Sauce
1/2 cup mayonnaise
1 tsp. seasoning salt
1-1/2 cups of cooked shrimp, lobster or crabmeat

Place all vegetables into colander and pour 4 quarts of boiling water over them. Allow to drain. Mix pasta and blanched vegetables. Mix Lea & Perrins, mayonnaise and seasoning salt until thoroughly blended. Fold into pasta mixture. Add seafood and mix well. Chill before serving.

Serves 4.

Salad Nicoise

Ocean Resources Branch
State of Hawaii Department of Business
and Economic Development

3/4 lb. Hawaiian Tombo (Albacore Tuna)
1 small head Romaine lettuce
1/2 lb. green beans, blanched and cut into 2 inch lengths
3 new potatoes, cooked and sliced
1 large carrot, peeled and cut into julienne strips
1 small cucumber, sliced
1 tomato, cut into wedges
2 hard cooked eggs, sliced
1/4 cup red wine vinegar
1 tsp. Diijon mustard
1/2 tsp. salt
1/8 tsp. pepper
1/2 cup olive oil
2 Tbs. vegetable oil
2 thinly sliced Anchovy fillets
Olives
Capers

Remove skin and bones from tombo fillet, cut into cubes
or slices and set aside. Line a serving platter with lettuce
leaves. Arrange the green beans, potatoes, carrot, cucumber,
tomatoes and eggs on the lettuce leaves. Make a dressing by
combining red wine vinegar, mustard, salt and pepper.
Slowly add olive oil, beating continually, until well blended.
Lightly saute tombo in vegetable oil until cooked and place
in center of salad. Top with anchovies. Garnish with olives
and capers.

Serves 4.

Fresh Ahi Salad

Kris Smith

1 lb. ahi; baked, chilled and cubed
1/4 cup crumbled blue cheese
3 Tbs. white wine vinegar
1 Tbs. olive oil
1 tsp. Dijon mustard
1/4 tsp. dill weed
1/8 tsp. ground black pepper
1 head Manoa lettuce
1 head Romaine lettuce

Wash and tear lettuce into bite size pieces. Arrange on four plates. Arrange cubed ahi in center of each plate. Beat well remaining ingredients and pour over salads.

Serves 4.

Scallop Pasta Salad

Kris Smith

1/2 lb. scallops, poached in wine and chilled
1/4 lb. fresh linguine, cooked and cut into 6 inch lengths
1 small can mandarin oranges, drained
2 Tbs. minced green onion
1/4 cup white wine vinegar
2 Tbs. olive oil
1 tsp. orange jest
3/4 tsp. dry mustard
Dash white pepper
1/2 lb. Chinese peas, steamed
1 red pepper, seeded and julienned
1/4 cup toasted slivered almonds

Combine scallops, pasta, oranges and green onion. Beat well vinegar, oil, jest, mustard and white pepper. Pour over scallop mixture, cover and refrigerate overnight. Just before serving, stir in peas and top with almonds.

Serves 4.

Poached Scallop Salad with Basil Dressing

Kris Smith

1/2 lb. scallops
1 cup dry white wine
Juice of one lemon
1 head Manoa lettuce
1 tomato, cut into six wedges
6 asparagus spears, steamed and chilled
1 avocado, peeled and sliced

Dressing:

Whip together 6 Tbs. olive oil, 3 Tbs. white wine vinegar, one clove garlic (minced) and 1/2 tsp. each dry mustard, seasoning salt, and dry basil. Stir in a dash of nutmeg.

Heat wine and lemon juice in a small saucepan. Add scallops and simmer 5 minutes or until cooked. Remove with slotted spoon and cool. Tear lettuce into bite size pieces and arrange on two plates. Divide scallops in half and arrange in center of lettuce bed. Garnish with tomato wedges, asparagus spears and avocado slices. Top with dressing and serve.

Serves 2.

Tropical Shrimp Salad

Kris Smith

1 lb. large shrimp or prawns
1 cup white wine
1 cup water
1 small onion, chopped
2 stalks lemon grass, chopped
1 head Manoa lettuce
1 ripe mango, cubed
2 Tbs. macadamia nut bits
2 Tbs. minced green onions

Dressing:

Whip together one small egg yolk, 1 Tbs. lime juice, 1 tsp. lemon juice, 1 tsp. orange juice and 1/2 tsp. honey. Add 1/4 cup olive oil and seasoning salt and pepper to taste. Whisk.

In a small saucepan, heat wine, water, onion and lemon grass. When mixture simmers, add shrimp and simmer covered for 10 minutes. Remove shrimp, peel and chill. Arrange lettuce on two plates. Toss chilled shrimp, mango, nuts, green onion and dressing until thoroughly coated. Arrange on lettuce bed and serve.

Serves 2.

Entrees

Fish in Parchment Serendipity

Bones Yuen, Chef
Serendipity

18" X 36" parchment paper, folded in half
8 oz. fillet of fish, soft kind—Opakapaka or Mahimahi
1-1/2 oz. Sauterne wine
1 Tbs. butter
1 shallot, sliced
2 heaping tsp. capers
3 oz. bay shrimp
1 Tbs. chopped parsley

Place fish on center of paper, crosswise, top with remaining items. Bring flaps A together and fold and crease. Fold two more times. Crimp and twist one of the B sides. Pour in open side the Sauterne wine. Crimp and fold other B side. Bake in hot oven (400-500°) for 7-10 minutes in a pan.

One serving.

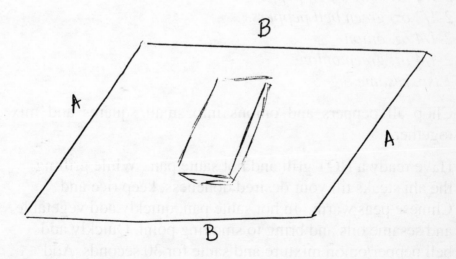

Grilled Island Ahi with Szechuan Style Shrimp

Roy Yamaguchi, Owner and Chef
Roy's Restaurant

14 oz. steamed Chinese peas and steamed rice

4 (7 oz.) Ahi steaks
1 tsp. fresh ginger, minced
1 tsp. fresh garlic, minced
2 oz. vegetable oil

Coat ahi evenly with ginger, garlic and oil.

15 shrimp (16/20 size), chopped
1/2 tsp. Garlic Chili Paste
1/2 tsp. mushroom soy sauce

Combine chopped shrimp with garlic, chili paste, and
mushroom soy. Reserve for 30 minutes.

2-1/2 oz. red bell peppers
2-1/2 oz. yellow bell peppers
2-1/2 oz. green bell peppers
2-1/4 oz. onion
2-1/4 oz. green onion
1 tsp. sesame oil

Chop all peppers and onions into small squares and mix
together.

Have ready a HOT grill and hot saute pan. While grilling
the ahi steaks till your desired doneness, keep rice and
Chinese peas warm. In hot saute pan, quickly add vegetable
and sesame oils and bring to smoking point. Quickly add
bell pepper/onion mixture and saute for 30 seconds. Add

marinated shrimp and saute for 15 additional seconds, stirring constantly. Remove from heat.

Place Chinese peas in middle of each plate. Place ahi on top of peas. Spoon bell pepper and shrimp mixture over each ahi steak. Serve immediately with steamed rice.

Serves 4.

Broiled Opakapaka, Filled with Black Olives, In a Light Seafood Sauce

Executive Chef Philippe Padovani
La Mer, Halekulani

Ingredients for Broiled Opakapaka:
2 lb. Opakapaka, 8 oz. per person
8 Black Olives, pitted
2 oz. Olive Oil, to coat fillet before broiling

Ingredients for Nage of Aromatics:
1 pint white wine
1/2 pint water
4 oz. carrots, chopped
4 oz. onions, chopped
2-1/2 oz. shallots, chopped
2-1/2 oz. celery with leaves, chopped
2 whole cloves of garlic
2 whole cloves (spice)
1 bouquet of herbs-bay leaf, parsley and thyme
1/2 lemon, sliced
1/2 oz. salt
Dash of white pepper with a pinch of cayenne pepper

Ingredients for Seafood Sauce:
8 oz. Finished Nage of Aromatics
2 oz. Olive Oil
2 oz. shallots, chopped
5 medium tomatoes
*6 oz. chopped herbs-chives, tarragon, chervil, seaweed and
    parsley*
2 oz. butter
1/2 lemon, juiced
Salt and pepper to taste

First, prepare the nage of aromatics, then the seafood sauce, followed by the fish fillets. Have fish cleaned and scaled, and removing all the bones in advance; or purchase the fish already cleaned and cut into fillets.

Method for Nage of Aromatics:
Bring water and wine to a boil. Add the chopped vegetables, aromatic herbs and lemon juice. Continue to boil for 30 minutes. Half way through, add salt and pepper. At the end of the cooking process, strain the mixture through a fine sieve, set the clear liquid aside to cool and discard the rest of the ingredients.

Method for Seafood Sauce:
Begin by blanching the tomatoes. Cut fine lines from top to bottom, just deep enough to cut the skin and drop tomatoes in rapidly boiling water. After 30 seconds, drain and run under cold water until tomatoes are cool enough to handle. Peel skin off, cut in half and remove seeds. Finish by dicing.

In a frying pan, combine diced tomatoes, shallots and olive oil. Simmer slowly until shallots turn clear, about 5 minutes. Add nage of aromatics, lemon juice, butter and mixed herbs. Mix with a whisk and continue to simmer for 5 min. over medium heat. Correct seasoning to taste, remove from heat and set aside.

Method for Opakapaka:
Preheat oven to 500°. Fish should be cleaned in advance.

Continued on next page

With tip of knife, pierce eight holes in the fish fillets.

Cut 8 pitted olives lengthwise in fours. Stuff one in each hole.

Coat both sides of fillet with olive oil and place on broiling pan. Cook for 3-5 min.

Remove from oven and place fillets on large dinner plates. Pour 4 oz. of seafood sauce over each. Serve while hot.

Serves 4.

Onaga Lau Lau

Executive Chef Alois Raidl

6 oz. Onaga filet (deboned)
2 shrimp (13/15)
2 scallops (jumbo)
10 oz. fresh spinach
2 Ti leaves
2 T. Sesame oil
Salt
Pepper

Sauce:
1/4 c. sesame seed oil
1 t. sesame seed
1 T. green onions (diced)
2 T. white wine vinegar
1 t. fresh ginger (grated)
1 t. fresh garlic (chopped fine)
1/2 c. shoyu
2 T. sugar

Combine all sauce ingredients in pot except green onions.
Bring to boil, then cool. Add in green onions. Spoon over
onaga before serving.

Preparation of onaga: Divide spinach equally into 2 beds.
Place onaga on a bed of spinach then place shrimp and
scallops over onaga. Drizzle 2 tablespoons sesame oil, salt
and pepper to taste.

Place other bed of spinach over Onaga. Wrap with ti leaves.
Steam for 20 minutes.

Serves 2

Oven Roasted Opakapaka

Executive Chef David Turner
The Black Orchid

6 - 6 oz. opakapaka filets
4 c. basmati rice
1 c. basil leaves
1/2 lb. whole butter, room temperature
2 c. sour cream
1 t. saffron or tumeric
1/2 c. lime juice
1 T. half and half
Salt and pepper
Peanut oil
Grilled vegetables for garnish (eggplant, tomato, zucchini,
*   etc.)*

Preheat oven to 450°. Rinse rice then place in heavy pot.
Cover with 1/2" of water. Place on high heat and boil until
liquid is gone. Turn off heat. Cover and let stand 15 minutes.

Take 1/2 portion of basil and chop in processor. Add butter
and run until smooth. Reserve.

Take saffron and lime juice in small pan (heat over red
flame) and reduce to 2 tablespoons. Cool.

In processor, combine 1 c. sour cream with saffron
reduction. Run until even yellow color. Add pinch of salt
and thin with half and half. Can be made one day in
advance, store in refrigerator.

Take remaining basil and chop in processor. Add 1 cup of
sour cream and 1 tablespoon of lime juice. Mix until

smooth. Add pinch of salt and thin with half and half. Can be made one day in advance, store in refrigerator.

Season fillets with salt and pepper. Heat peanut oil in heavy oven-proof fry pan. Brown fish (skin side up) then flip and brown skin side. Drain oil and place pan in 450° oven. Fish should take 4-8 minutes to finish. DO NOT OVER COOK!

Transfer rice to large bowl and toss with basil butter until all grains are coated. Season with salt and pepper.

Arrange vegetables on perimeter of plate or platter. Mound rice in center and place cooked filets on rice. Drizzle each sauce over fish.

Serves 6.

Fillet of Hawaiian Sunfish

Executive Chef Detlef Greiert
Maile Restaurant, Kahala Hilton

Fillets (2):
1 Hawaiian sunfish (8-10 oz.)
Salt and pepper
1/2 oz. butter
2 oz. fish stock

Lobster Dumplings:
1 frozen lobster tail
1-1/2 oz. fresh spinach leaves
Salt and pepper
2 oz. fish stock (optional)

Saffron Sauce:
1 cup cream
1/2 cup white wine
1 cup fish stock
Pinch saffron
2 Tbs. sweet butter
Salt and pepper
Dash Pernod

Finishing:
Black linguine
Chervil
Salmon eggs
2 Lobster or crab claws, cooked

Fillets:
Filet sunfish and clean completely of all small bones. Use
one filet per portion. Season with salt and pepper. Butter pan
or dish to be used for poaching, put in fish, cover with fish
stock and poach.

Lobster Dumplings:

Cook lobster tail to medium doneness. But into 6 pieces 3/4 inch each and season with salt and pepper. Clean spinach leaves well and lightly blanche in boiling water. Immediately transfer leaves to bowl of ice water to keep them a nice fresh green color. Wrap lobster pieces in spinach leaves, then wrap in plastic wrap, sealing tightly and forming a small ball. Steam dumplings until heated thoroughly or poach slowly in fish stock in a covered pot.

Saffron Sauce:

Combine cream, white wine and fish stock and reduce to half. Add Pernod and saffron. Slowly whip in butter. Season with salt and pepper.

Finishing:

Cook linguine (or any other pasta) al dente in salt water. Saute in melted fresh sweet butter and season to taste with salt only.

Place saffron sauce on plate, covering entire surface. On the sauce, arrange the linguine, 3 lobster dumplings and one of the sunfish fillets. Garnish lobster dumplings with salmon eggs and fish fillet with a sprig of chervil. Place vegetables next to the linguine (asparagus tips and carrots are suggested). Top the linguine with a lobster or crab claw.

Serves 2.

Opakapaka With Red Curry Sauce

Keo's Thai Cuisine Restaurant

2 pounds filet opakapaka
2 tablespoon rice flour
Oil for deep frying
1/2 small head cabbage, chopped
1/4 cup oil
Red Curry Paste, recipe follows
1 cup coconut milk
4 teaspoon nam pla (fish sauce)
10-15 fresh basil leaves

Clean fish. Lightly coat with rice flour. Make a series of cuts one half inch apart along both sides of fish. Heat oil for frying to 350°. Fry fish for 15 minutes or until done, being careful not to overcook. Line a serving platter with chopped cabbage and place cooked fish on top. Set aside. Heat the 1/4 cup vegetable oil over medium heat and saute Red Curry Paste for 3 minutes. Stir in coconut milk and cook for 2 minutes. Reduce heat to medium-low and stir in fish sauce and basil. Cook for 3 minutes. Pour over fish.

Serves 4.

Thai Red Curry Paste:
1 bulb garlic, minced
6 shallots, minced
12 small red chili peppers
1 stalk lemon grass, thinly sliced
1/2 teaspoon Chinese parsley (coriander) seeds
1 bunch Chinese parsley, root ends

Combine all ingredients and grind in food processor or in a mortar.

Fish With Caper Sauce

Martin Wyss
Swiss Inn

Fish (8 pieces, 3 ounces each)
Salt
Flour
Au Jus
Unsalted butter
Lemon
Capers
Chopped parsley

Season fish with salt and dust lightly with flour. Heat butter or oil in a skillet and saute fish slowly, being careful not to brown too much. When fish is almost cooked, remove filets. Discard excess oil and place fish back into pan. Add some au jus, lemon juice, unsalted butter, capers and chopped parsley. Cook until sauce becomes a little creamy. Remove filets and arrange on serving platter. Pour sauce over fish. Serve with parsley potatoes and vegetables. Garnish with lemon wedge and parsley.

Serves 4.

Barbecued Swordfish Fillets

Jeff Kissel

For each 1/2 lb. of swordfish, combine the following:

2 Tbs. fresh lemon juice
1/4 tsp. freshly grated ginger
1/2 clove minced garlic
1/4 tsp. coarsely ground pepper
2 tsp. French's mustard

Coat thick swordfish fillets with this mixture and allow to marinate for no more than fifteen minutes. Scrape off excess marinade and combine with 4 Tbs. of Olive Oil for each 1/2 lb. of swordfish to create a basting sauce. Grill swordfish over medium hot coals for approximately 10 minutes per side, basting often.

Barbecued Salmon

Iris McGivern

1/4 cup fresh apple cider
1/4 cup soy sauce
2 Tbs. unsalted butter
1 large clove garlic, crushed
2 salmon fillets, 2-1/2-3 lb. each or 5 lb. salmon steaks, cut
    about 1 inch thick
Sprigs of fresh parsley or coriander and lemon slices for
    garnish.

In a small saucepan, combine cider and soy sauce. Bring
to boil over high heat, reduce heat and simmer for a few
minutes. Add butter and garlic and continue cooking, stirring
occasionally until the liquid thickens enough to coat the
back of a spoon—about 20 minutes. Remove from heat and
cool to room temperature. Pat fillets dry and place them
skin-side down on a rack. Brush the marinade evenly over
fillets, and let stand at room temperature for 30 minutes.

When coals of barbecue are hot, oil your rack and place
the fillets skin-side down on the grill. Tent with aluminum
foil and "bake" until the flesh is slightly translucent in the
thickest part, roughly 15-20 minutes. It is not recommended
to turn the fillet as you run the risk of breaking the fillet.

Serve garnished with parsley and lemon slices.

To cook salmon indoors: Preheat broiler. Place salmon
skin-side down on a well oiled broiler rack and broil about
6 inches from the heat until the top is glazed and the fish is
slightly translucent in the center-12-15 minutes.

Serves 2.

Fish With Saffron Sauce

Martin Wyss
Swiss Inn

Saffron
Fish (8 pieces - 3 ounces each)
White Wine
Salt
Pepper
Flour
Unsalted Butter
Chopped Shallots
Tomato, seeded and diced
Cucumber, peeled, seeded and diced
Heavy Cream

Heat skillet slightly; add butter. Add shallots and a little chopped saffron. Place fish on shallots and sprinkle cucumbers and tomatoes around fish. Add wine; cover and simmer slowly. When cooked, remove fish, tomatoes and cucumbers and arrange on platter. Reduce liquid; add heavy cream and reduce. Whip in butter. Season to taste and pour over fish. Serve immediately.

Serves 4.

Shoyu Marlin

Betty Jo Thompson

3 slices marlin, 3/4 inch thick
1/4 cup lemon juice
1/4 cup shoyu sauce
2 ounces red wine
1 teaspoon grated fresh ginger
1/4 teaspoon garlic powder
1 teaspoon sugar
3-4 drops sesame oil
1/4 cup chopped green onion

Place fish in baking dish in single layer. Pour lemon juice
over fish. Marinate for 30 minutes or more. Cover dish with
plastic wrap. Cook in microwave oven for 2 minutes on
High. Let rest 2 minutes. Cook on High for an additional
2 minutes. Let stand until sauce is cooled. Place balance
of ingredients in microwave dish and cook on High for
2 minutes. Pour sauce over marlin and serve.

Serves 3.

Red Snapper A La Veracruz

Sybille Char

4 red snapper fillets
Juice of one lime
Salt and pepper
1 chili pepper, thinly sliced
2 medium onions, thinly sliced
2 cloves garlic, minced
1/4 cup olive oil
3 medium tomatoes, peeled, seeded and chopped
10 pimento stuffed green olives, halved
2 Tbs. capers
Corn Meal

Marinate the fish fillets in the lime juice, salt and pepper for
1-2 hours in the refrigerator. Heat oven to 350°.

Saute onions and garlic in olive oil until onion is transparent.
Stir in tomatoes, olives, capers and chili pepper. Simmer
10 minutes.

Drain fillets and dust lightly with corn meal. Arrange fillets
in a single layer in a baking dish. Spoon tomato mixture
over fillets. Bake fish 10-15 minutes or until fish flakes.
Serve with hot rice.

Serves 4.

Ahi Fillets with Shallots and Raspberry Vinegar Sauce

Kathi Dildy

1/3 cup raspberry vinegar
2 Tbs. finely minced shallots
1 stick butter or margarine
2 Ahi fillets
Lemon pepper
Paprika

Combine vinegar and shallots in a small saucepan. Bring to a boil, lower heat slightly and simmer until vinegar is reduced to 2 Tbs. Whisk in 1 stick butter or margine. Sauce will thicken slightly.

Sprinkle fillets with lemon pepper and paprika on both sides. Saute in a small amount of butter or margarine until done, being careful not to overcook.

Serve with the raspberry vinegar sauce and rice.

Serves 2

Steamed Fish with Lup Cheong and Tau See

Hannah and Jimbo Beaumont

1 to 2 lb. mullet/Opakapaka/Onaga, your favorite—whole, cleaned and scaled
1 tsp. sugar
1 tsp. salt
1 Tbs. sherry
1 Tbs. shoyu
3 Tbs. peanut oil
1 Tbs. salad oil
1 Tbs. Tau See, mashed
1 Tbs. minced fresh ginger
1 Tbs. crushed garlic
Green onion, minced
Yellow onion, chopped
Lup Cheong

Combine sugar, salt, sherry and shoyu. Rub inside and outside of fish. Let fish sit for twenty minutes. Stuff fish with lup cheong and chopped onion. Place fish in shallow baking dish; top with any remaining sauce, salad oil, green onion, garlic, ginger and tau see. Steam for 20 minutes. Heat peanut oil and pour over fish. Transfer to serving platter, garnish with cilantro and serve.

Serves 3-4.

Mom's Ono Fried Fish

Lurline Degagne

This recipe is ideal for fish 3 lb. or more like Uhu. Deep fry fish until crispy, golden brown and done. Set aside on large platter.

For each 3 lb. of fish:

Marinate 1/2 lb. of cut up pork in 1/3 cup shoyu, 1 large clove minced garlic; and 1 tsp. each of minced ginger, sugar and ground pepper. Clean and chop into one inch lengths about 3/4 lb. of string beans and slice one medium round onion. Heat a few tablespoons of oil in saucepan. Add pork and stir until cooked. Add string beans, onion and one 14 oz. can of chicken broth. Stir in 2 Tbs. oyster sauce and salt to taste. Thicken with a tablespoon or so of cornstarch mixed with equal amounts of water. Pour thickened sauce over cooked fish and serve hot.

Serves 4-6.

Note: mustard cabbage, round onion and tomato wedges can be substituted for string beans and onion.

Poached Fish with Seafood Sauce

Kris Smith

2 lbs. fish fillets
1/4 cup cold water
1 Tbs. cornstarch
2 small green onion, minced
1 tsp. minced garlic
1/4 lb. fresh scallops
1/4 lb. medium shrimp
1-6 oz. can crabmeat
1/4 cup dry white wine
1-1/2 cup half and half
2 tsp. lemon juice
Salt and pepper to taste
Wine for poaching

Arrange fillets in shallow pan and add enough wine to almost cover. Simmer on stove top until fish is opaque, turning once. Set aside.

In small bowl, mix water with cornstarch until smooth. In small saucepan, saute green onion and garlic in 1 tablespoon margarine for a few minutes, set aside. Peel and devein shrimp and slice in half lengthwise. Cut up scallops so they are in 1/2 inch pieces. Drain crabmeat. Return sauteed onion and garlic to medium heat and add scallops and shrimp. Cook, stirring frequently, for two minutes. With slotted spoon, remove seafood to separate plate. To saucepan add wine and half and half. Heat to boiling. Reduce heat to medium and continue to cook, stirring constantly for an additional five minutes. Stir in cornstarch mixture and simmer over low heat until sauce begins to thicken. Stir in lemon juice, scallops, shrimp and crabmeat. Season with salt and pepper.

Arrange fish fillets on bed of fresh cooked linguini and top with sauce.

Serves 4.

Salmon Steak Micro Rave

Nancy Watton-Murphy

4-6 Salmon steaks, about 3/4 inch thick
2 Tbs. butter or margarine
1 tsp. dill weed
1 Tbs. Vermouth

Rinse and pat salmon steaks dry. Place butter and dill weed in a 7 by 11 inch microwave dish. Microwave on High uncovered for 30 seconds or until butter melts. Stir in Vermouth. Place steaks in dish and turn to coat. Cover with waxed paper. Microwave on High for 3 minutes. Turn salmon steaks over, recover with waxed paper and microwave for 3-5 minutes more or until salmon flakes with a fork.

Serves 4-6.

Baked Salmon

Evarts Fox

1 whole (6 lb.) salmon
2 lemons, sliced
2 onions, sliced
10-12 whole peppercorns
2 cups dry white wine

Place in large roasting pan a large piece of cheesecloth that extends over edge of pan. This will enable you to lift fish from pan when done. Stuff fish cavity with half of the lemon and onion slices and half the pepper-corns. Place remaining lemon slices, onion and peppercorns on top of fish. Pour wine over fish. Bake for 45-60 minutes at 350°. Serve warm or chilled with cucumber sauce.

Serves 8.

Cucumber sauce:
1 cucumber, chilled and seeded
2 Tbs. mayonnaise
1/2 cup sour cream or yogurt
2 Tbs. fresh lemon juice
Dill weed to taste
Salt and pepper to taste

Grate cucumber or shred in food processor. Drain on paper towels. Mix with remaining ingredients. Serve with baked salmon.

Spooner's Foil Fish

Cynthia Haws

2 A'u steaks
Mayonnaise
8-10 thinly sliced mushrooms
2 Tbs. capers
1 small Maui onion, thinly sliced in rings
2 Tbs. lemon juice
Lemon pepper

Preheat oven to 375°. Place fish in the center of a piece of foil large enough to wrap it and all the other ingredients. Slather mayonnaise on top of each piece of fish. Layer mushrooms, onions and capers on top of fish. Sprinkle with lemon juice and lemon pepper. Fold foil over fish and fold over the sides to make a roughly rectangular package, crimping the edges. Place on a cookie sheet or shallow baking pan in oven. Bake for 15 minutes. Unfold seams. If fish is not quite done, bake longer with the foil partially folded back so you can check for doneness easily and frequently.

Serves 2.

Smoked Salmon and Scrambled Eggs

Mary Batterham

4 eggs
1 oz. butter
Dash of milk
Salt and Pepper
Dash of Worcestershire sauce
Lemon Juice / Capers / Black Pepper
2 toasted bagels
3 oz. smoked salmon

Break eggs into bowl; add milk, salt and pepper and
Worcestershire sauce. Beat eggs with milk. Heat frying pan,
melt butter, add eggs and scramble. When cooked to desired
doneness, top bagels with eggs. Cover with smoked salmon.
Garnish with black pepper, capers and lemon juice.

Serves 2.

Curried Fish Sticks

Dorothy Brockhausen

1 lb. Red Snapper fillets
1 egg, beaten

Crumb mixture:
1/2 cup corn flake crumbs
1/8 cup flour
1/8 cup corn meal
1/2 teaspoon Garlic Salt
1/8 teaspoon freshly ground Pepper
1/8 teaspoon Curry Powder

Oil for frying

Remove any bones from fillets. Cut fillets into 1 inch wide strips. Blend together well all crumb mixture ingredients. Dip fish strips into beaten egg and then into crumb mixture to coat. Heat oil and fry strips until browned on one side. Turn carefully and brown on second side. Serve with tartar sauce.

Serves 3.

Shrimp Dijon

Doris Harrison

Juice of one lemon
2 lb. raw shrimp
4 Tbs. melted butter
2 Tbs. oil
1 Tbs. Dijon mustard
4-6 cloves garlic, minced
1/2 tsp. Worcestershire sauce

Mix together all ingredients, let stand in refrigerator for a minimum of two hours. Broil at 450° for 5 minutes or until done.

Serves 8.

Prawns in Spicy Tomato Sauce

Mary Batterham

2 lbs. prawns
4 cloves of garlic, crushed
1/2 inch fresh ginger, grated
1 tsp. fresh chilies, minced
4 Tbs. olive oil
Pinch each of basil and oregano
2 cans of whole tomatoes
1 glass of white wine

Heat 2 tablespoons of oil in large saucepan. Saute garlic and ginger. Add chilies and cook for one minute. Add tomatoes, juice and all. Cook for a few minutes. Add basil and oregano, salt and pepper to taste. Add wine, cover and cook slowly until sauce thickens. Peel and devein prawns. Fry in remaining oil until pink (do not overcook). Pour tomato sauce over prawns and serve on a bed of cooked pasta with french bread.

Serves 4.

Oysters à la Grace

Garrett Grace

4 soft tomatoes, chopped
1 red bell pepper, sliced in rings
1 zucchini, sliced
1 onion, chopped
3-4 mushrooms, sliced
2 cloves garlic, minced
1 can of smoked oysters
Cooked pasta
1 Tbs. olive oil
Red wine

Saute vegetables in olive oil. When they are soft, add smoked oysters and season with red wine to taste. Simmer for five minutes and serve with pasta.

Serves 2.

Kimopino

Warner "Kimo" Sutton

1/4 cup Extra Virgin Olive Oil
2 Tbs. sweet butter
3 cups chopped Maui onions
1/3 cup chopped scallions
1 each green, red and gold peppers, cut into 2 inch strips
2-3 leeks, trimmed and chopped
5-7 cloves garlic, pressed or crushed
4 stalks celery, chopped
2 carrots, sliced
4 cups plum tomatoes, peeled and chopped
8 oz. mushrooms
2 oz. Brandy
1 cup V-8 juice
2 tsp. Thai fish sauce
1 6 oz. can tomato paste
12 oz. Black Pasta-Squid Ink (broken)
1/2 cup fresh cut Basil
1 cup fresh minced Parsley
1 Tbs. Oregano
1 Tbs. Thyme
1-1/2 cup Limu
1-1/2 cup dry white wine (Soave)
1-1/2 cup sweet red wine (Marsala)
1-2 cup fish stock
1-2 cup bottled clam juice
4 green onions, chopped
2 tsp. sugar
2 Tbs. Worcestershire sauce
2 tsp. Saffron
Salt and Pepper
Grated peel and juice of 2 lemons

*1 lb. each Opakapaka, Mahimahi and Ahi-chopped into
    chunks
1/2 lb. smoked eel
1 lb. small calamari
1/2 lb. scallops
1-1/2 lb. shrimp
1-1/2 lb. Kahuku prawns
4 lb. clams
4 cooked Dungeness crabs
1-1/2 lb. Pacific lobster tails
2 cup shucked oysters
1 doz. mussels (optional)*

This is best if made one day ahead of time.

Heat olive oil in a kettle or large pot over medium-high heat
until hot. Add onions, scallions, peppers, leeks, celery,
carrots, garlic and spices (reserving 1/4 cup of parsley for
garnish). Simmer until onions are clear and peppers are
wilted. Add tomatoes, V-8 juice, tomato paste, wines and
clam juice. Salt and pepper to taste. Add herbs, fish stock
and Thai fish sauce. Stir, simmering 10 minutes. Add grated
lemon peel and lemon juice. Cool and refrigerate overnight
to blend flavors.

The next day, cook one hour longer to combine herbs and
broth, stirring often. Add black pasta. Heat to boiling.
Reduce heat. There are twenty-five minutes left before
serving. Add fish in the following order: eel, calamari,

Continued on next page

Opakapaka, Mahimahi, and Ahi. Cover pot and simmer five minutes. If you are having french bread with dinner, pop it into the oven now. Next add prawns, shrimp and scallops. Stir and cover, allow to simmer 3-5 minutes. Add brandy and mushrooms and stir in lobster chucks, mussels, clams and oysters. Crack crab and add to pot. Simmer 5 minutes or until clams open. Add limu. Ladle into a large soup tureen or directly into large soup bowls. Garnish with remaining parsley. Serve immediately with hot french bread. Other good garnishes are red pepper flakes and freshly grated Parmesan cheese. Chardonnay goes especially well with this dish.

Serves 10–12.

Fettucini Sharp

Jim Sharp

1-1/2 cup heavy cream
1-1/2 cup freshly grated Parmesan cheese
1/2 cup butter
2 egg yolks
White pepper
Seasoning salt
1 6 oz. can crabmeat, drained
1 cup imitation crabmeat, cut into chunks
1/4 lb. fresh asparagus, steamed and sliced into 2 inch
*   pieces*
1 lb. fresh fettucine noodles

Heat cream in a medium saucepan. When cream begins to simmer, stir in cheese, a little bit at a time. Continue stirring constantly over low heat for 10 minutes. Add the butter, 2 Tbs. at a time, until all butter is incorporated into the sauce and the texture is smooth. Remove from heat. Beat a small amount of sauce with the egg yolks. Return yolk mixture to the sauce, stirring thoroughly with a whisk. Fold in crabmeat and imitation crabmeat. Cook fettucine noodles and drain. Add to sauce and toss noodles until evenly coated. Fold in asparagus, season with seasoning salt and pepper and serve immediately.

Serves 6

Fresh Clam Sauce/Iidako Sauce

Maggie Parkes

1 2-lb. can Italian plum tomatoes
1 medium onion, chopped
5 cloves garlic, chopped
1 bunch Chinese parsley, chopped
1 package of fresh basil, chopped
1 chopped jalapeno pepper (optional)
1/3 cup olive oil
Salt, pepper and thyme to taste

Saute onions, garlic and jalapeno gently in olive oil until transparent. Add tomatoes, coarsely chopped, plus half of the chopped parsley and basil. Simmer about one half hour, adding a little water or white wine if sauce becomes too "dry". Season with salt, pepper and thyme. This is the basic tomato sauce. Mix this with the following ingredients.

2 cans chopped clams, drained
1 can flat fillets of anchovy
1-1/2 lb. fresh manilla clams (small ones are sweeter)
Balance of parsley and basil from above
Pinch of saffron (optional but recommended)

Add the 2 cans of clams to the basic sauce. Bring to a strong simmer. Add anchovies, mix in- they will disintegrate. Add parsley and basil. Lastly add manilla clams and simmer until they open. Serve with pasta.

To make Iidako Sauce:

Make basic tomato sauce. In a skillet saute quickly and briefly on high heat:

1 lb. baby squid (iidako), chopped coarsely
1/3 cup olive oil
Several cloves garlic, chopped

Add to tomato sauce, oil and all. Serve over pasta.

Serves 6-8.

Clam Sauce with Linguini

Debbie Simpson

2 cans minced clams
3 cloves garlic, minced
1 small onion, chopped
1/3 cup olive oil
2 Tbs. butter
1 tsp. crumbled oregano
1/2 tsp. salt
1/8 tsp. pepper
8 oz. La Rosa brand linguini, cooked
2 Tbs. chopped parsley
1 tsp. grated lemon rind
2 Tbs. lemon juice
Grated fresh Parmesan cheese

Drain clams, reserving juice. Saute onion and garlic in oil and butter for 5 minutes. Add clam juice, oregano, salt and pepper. Bring to a boil over high heat, continue to boil for about five minutes or until mixture reduces to 1 cup. Add clams, parsley, lemon rind and juice. Add noodles and toss until thoroughly coated. Sprinkle with Parmesan.

Serves 3-4.

Creamy Clam and Pesto Sauce

Serafina Smith

1 cup chopped fresh basil leaves
1/4 cup chopped fresh parsley
1 can minced clams, drained
2 cloves garlic, crushed
3 Tbs. extra virgin olive oil
3 Tbs. freshly grated Parmesan cheese

Add all ingredients to food processor or blender, with the exception of the clams. Blend on high speed for a minute. If mixture is too dry, add a few tablespoons of warm water. Fold in clams. Toss with cooked pasta.

Serves 2–3.

Tuna Tacos

Nancy Watton Murphy

1 can tuna, drained
1/4 cup mayonnaise
1/4 cup Italian salad dressing
1/2 head shredded lettuce
1 tomato, chopped
One dozen corn tortillas, fried and shaped into taco shells

Mix first five ingredients. Fill taco shells. Enjoy!

Serves 6.

Tuna-Rice Casserole

Karla Vasey

2 cups of cooked rice
2 eggs
2 cups milk
1 can cream of mushroom soup
1 can tuna
1 cup toasted wheat germ

Beat eggs with milk. Mix with mushroom soup and blend
thoroughly. Fold in tuna and cooked rice. Butter a casserole
and sprinkle bottom with half of wheat germ. Pour in
tuna-rice mixture. Sprinkle balance of wheat germ evenly
over top of casserole. Bake uncovered at 350° for about
one hour.

Serves 8.

Seafood Curry

Aaron Young

3 teaspoon Curry Powder
1/2 pound butter
3 cloves chopped garlic
1/2 pound Mahi Mahi
1/2 pound imitation crab
1/2 pound shrimp
1/2 pound scallops
1 pound carrots
1 pound potatoes
1 - 10 ounce jar oysters
3 cans Cream of Mushroom soup
Bay Leaf

Chop seafood and vegetables into bite sized pieces. Parboil carrots and potatoes and set aside. In a large pot, saute shrimp in 1/4 pound butter and garlic. When shrimp is done, blend in Cream of Mushroom soup and 3 teaspoons Curry Powder and Bay Leaf. Set aside and stir occasionally. In a separate skillet, saute scallops, mahi mahi and oysters in remaining butter. Stir in crab, carrots and potatoes. Mix with Cream of Mushroom soup. Heat thoroughly and serve.

Serves 6.

Crab-Broccoli Casserole

Joy Weeman

1 6 oz. package crab meat
1 pkg. frozen broccoli
1 cup grated cheddar cheese
1/4 cup margarine
2 Tbs. minced onion
2 Tbs. flour
1/8 tsp. curry powder
1/2 tsp. salt
1 cup milk
1 Tbs. lemon juice
2 Tbs. melted butter
1/2 cup soft bread crumbs

Cook broccoli and put in casserole dish. Sprinkle cheese over broccoli. Melt margarine and saute onions. Stir in flour, curry powder and salt. Stir in milk. Cook over low until thickened. Stir in lemon juice. Add crab meat. Pour over broccoli and cheese. Top with butter and bread crumbs. Bake at 350 degrees for 30 minutes.

Serves 4.

ALOHA

Glossary

GLOSSARY

AHI - The Yellowfin Tuna. Also known as Big Eye.

AJI NO MOTO - An oriental seasoning and tenderizer. Monosodium Glutamate.

AKU - The Skipjack Tuna.

A'U - The Hawaiian name for both the Striped Marlin (NAIRAGI) and the Blue Marlin (KAJIKI).

GARLIC CHILI PASTE - Sometimes called Chili Sauce with Garlic, a sauce made from red chili peppers. Found in the oriental food section.

HAPU'UPU'U - The Sea Bass or Grouper.

HEBI - The Spearfish.

IKA - Cuttlefish.

'INAMONA - Kukui Nut Paste.

LIMU - Seaweed.

LIMU-KOHU - A soft, succulent, small, red seaweed.

LOMI - To work or knead with your hands.

LUP CHEONG - a type of Chinese sausage.

MANAUWEA (OGO) - A small, crunchy, red, stick-like type of seaweed.

ONAGA - The Red Snapper.

ONO - A type of fish also known as the Wahoo.

OPAH - The Moonfish

OPAKAPAKA - The Pink Snapper.

OYSTER SAUCE - Sauce made from the extract of oysters. Found in oriental food section.

SAKE - Japanese rice wine.

SHIITAKI - Japanese mushrooms.

SHOYU - Soy sauce.

TAMARIND - A small preserved fruit. Found in the oriental food section.

TAU SEE - Oriental black beans.

THAI FISH SAUCE - Sauce made from Anchovy extract. Found in oriental food section. Also known as Nam Pla.

TOMBO - The Albacore Tuna.

UKU - The Grey Snapper.

ULUA - A type of fish also known as the Jack.

WASABI - Japanese horseradish. Found in oriental food
section.

YAKI NORI - Dried sheets of seaweed used in making sushi
rolls. Found in the oriental food section.

Index

Ahi Fillets with Shallots and
  Raspberry Vinegar Sauce 73
Baked Salmon 79
Barbecued Salmon 69
Barbecued Swordfish Fillets 68
Bon's Blackened Fish 22
Bouillabaisse, Hawaiian Style 38
Broiled Opakapaka, Filled with Black Olives, In a Light
  Seafood Sauce 58
Calamari Provencal for Two 15
Celery Seed Dressing 41
Clam Sauce with Linguini 92
Crab Dip 7
Crab Soup 33
Crab Spread 14
Crab, Macaroni and Potato Salad 46
Crab-Broccoli Casserole 97
Creamy Clam and Pesto Sauce 93
Curried Fish Sticks 82
Dilled Shrimp Spread 12
Fettucini Sharp 89
Fillet of Hawaiian Sunfish 64
Fish in Parchment Serendipity 55
Fish With Caper Sauce 67
Fish With Saffron Sauce 70
Fresh Ahi Salad 49
Fresh Clam Sauce/Iidako Sauce 90
Glossary 101
Grilled Island Ahi with Szechuan Style Shrimp 56
Hot Crab Dip 8
Ika Salad 45
Introduction 3

Kani No Nori Age Tempura 18
Kimopino 86
Limu Aku Poke 28
Lobster Bites 20
Lobster Rumaki 26
Mexican Shrimp Dip 11
Mom's Ono Fried Fish 75
New England Clam Chowder 35
Onaga Lau Lau 61
Ono Avocado and Crab Dip 9
Opakapaka With Red Curry Sauce 66
Order Blank 106
Oven Roasted Opakapaka 62
Oyster Stew 37
Oysters à la Grace 85
Pacific Broiler Grilled Shrimp and Scallops 16
Pasta Salad 47
Poached Fish with Seafood Sauce 76
Poached Scallop Salad with Basil Dressing 51
Poisson Cru 42
Prawns in Spicy Tomato Sauce 84
Red Ogo Salad 40
Red Snapper A La Veracruz 72
Ricotta Crabmeat Fritters 27
Royal Alii's Avocado Salad 39
Salad Nicoise 48
Salmon Pate 10
Salmon Spread 13
Salmon Steak Micro Rave 78
Scallop Pasta Salad 50
Scallop Seviche 43
Seafood Chowder 36

Seafood Curry 96
Seaside Chowder 34
Shark Bites 21
Shoyu Marlin 71
Shrimp Dijon 83
Smoked Salmon 29
Smoked Salmon and Scrambled Eggs 81
Spicy Shrimp 30
Spooner's Foil Fish 80
Steamed Fish with Lup Cheong and Tau See 74
Stuffed Mushrooms 23
Swedish Herring Salad 44
Tofu and Seasoned Clams 24
Tropical Shrimp Salad 52
Tuna Mold 25
Tuna Tacos 94
Tuna-Rice Casserole 95
Wok Magic Prawns 19

Notes:

Notes:

Notes:

Order Blank

I would like to order ___ copies of HAWAI'I'S CATCH OF THE DAY @ $7.95 each.

___ Enclosed please find my check. Charge my ___VISA ___ MASTERCARD

MasterCard Interbank No. _____ Expiration date _____

(No. above name on card)

Credit Card Number _____

Signature _____

Name _____

Address _____

City/State/Zip _____

Send to: Mutual Publishing
1127 11th Avenue Mezz. B
Honolulu, HI 96816

Phone: (808) 732-1709
Fax: (808) 734-4094

Join the Friends of the Hawai'i Maritime Center

Every member receives:

• Unlimited annual FREE admission to the Center for you and your immediate family.

•15% discount on everything in our unique gift shop.

•Your membership is tax deductible.

•You will have the satisfaction of knowing that you are helping to support numerous educational and vocational programs.

Hawai'i Maritime Center, Pier 7, Honolulu Harbor
Honolulu, HI 96813

Yes, I would like to join the Friends of Hawai'i Maritime Center.

___ Enclosed please find my check. Charge my ___VISA ___MASTERCARD

MasterCard Interbank No. _____ Expiration Date _____

(No. above name on card)

Credit Card Number _____

Signature _____

Name _____

Address _____

City/State/Zip _____

____ $35 Student/Senior ____ $50 Family ____ $100 First Mate

I'd like to donate more _____

Order Blank

I would like to order ___ copies of HAWAI'I'S CATCH OF THE DAY @ $7.95 each.

___ Enclosed please find my check. Charge my ___VISA ___ MASTERCARD

MasterCard Interbank No. _____ Expiration date _____

<small>(No. above name on card)</small>

Credit Card Number _____

Signature _____

Name _____

Address _____

City/State/Zip _____

Send to: Mutual Publishing   Phone: (808) 732-1709
1127 11th Avenue Mezz. B   Fax: (808) 734-4094
Honolulu, HI 96816

Join the Friends of the Hawai'i Maritime Center

Every member receives:

• Unlimited annual FREE admission to the Center for you and your immediate family.

•15% discount on everything in our unique gift shop.

•Your membership is tax deductible.

•You will have the satisfaction of knowing that you are helping to support numerous educational and vocational programs.

Hawai'i Maritime Center, Pier 7, Honolulu Harbor
Honolulu, HI 96813

Yes, I would like to join the Friends of Hawai'i Maritime Center.

___ Enclosed please find my check. Charge my ___VISA___MASTERCARD

MasterCard Interbank No. _____ Expiration Date _____

<small>(No. above name on card)</small>

Credit Card Number _____

Signature _____

Name _____

Address _____

City/State/Zip _____

____ $35 Student/Senior ____ $50 Family ____ $100 First Mate

I'd like to donate more _____